Songs of Miriam

A Women's Book of Devotions

Mary L. Mild, Editor

Songs of Miriam: A Women's Book of Devotions
© 1994
Judson Press, Valley Forge, PA 19482-0851

Bible quotations in this volume are from the NEW REVISED
STANDARD VERSION of the Bible, copyrighted 1989 by the
Division of Christian Education of the National Council of the
Churches of Christ in the United States of America, and are
used by permission. All rights reserved.

Library of Congress Cataloging-in-Publication Data
Songs of Miriam : a women's book of devotions / editor,
Mary L. Mild.
    p.   cm.
ISBN 0-8170-1207-9
1. Women—Prayer-books and devotions—English.
2. Spiritual life—Christianity. I. Mild, Mary L., 1944-
BV4844.S66 1994
242'.643—dc2093-45872

Printed in the U.S.A.

Table of Contents

Seasonal

Foreword

Meditation is in! Walk into any bookstore and one can find journaling books, books on spirituality, and the most popular series, *Meditations for Women Who Do Too Much.*

The contributors to *Songs of Miriam* have created this gem of a devotional book for women of faith who serve the church in many ways but perhaps do not take the time to reflect and renew themselves.

Songs of Miriam is written by gifted women from all arenas of church life. This devotional book contains both prose and poetry that is relevant to all parts of our lives: relationships, birth of a child, seeking out gifts from God, and especially understanding that we are created in God's image.

Do we women truly believe that we are created in God's image? Use this devotional book to understand the myriad ways God loves and supports us. This book celebrates women's gifts and their use in God's world.

Songs of Miriam reminds women of the importance of worshiping through daily and weekly reflection. The spiritual disciplines advise a daily exercise of prayer and reflection. This devotional, accompanied by reading of Scripture, is an effective resource for daily enrichment.

I hope that *Songs of Miriam* will be part of your way to focus on God through prayer and meditation.

Patricia J. Rumer
General Director
Church Women United
December 1993

Preface

"Then the prophet Miriam, Aaron's sister, took a tambourine in her hand; and all the women went out after her with tambourines and with dancing. And Miriam sang to them:

'Sing to the LORD, for he has triumphed gloriously; horse and rider he has thrown into the sea.' "
(*Exodus 15:20*)

We are blessed with a long tradition of women who have praised God. This book of devotions to God, written by women for women, is part of that never-ending tradition.

Miriam and the other women of Israel, having experienced God's saving power, could not contain themselves. They freely praised God with singing and dancing.

This book is filled with women's testimonies

to the mercies of God in their lives. You will be blessed as you experience these devotions and incorporate them with your own devotion to God.

Mary L. Mild
Valley Forge, Pennsylvania

Acknowledgments

The editor wishes to acknowledge with deep appreciation the contributions of Laura Alden, Ruth Ann Glover, Adalia Gutierrez-Lee and Debra Sutton, who have worked with her in producing this book.

Women and Worship

"Worship is a bridge across the gulf of silence into the land of deeds."—T. L. Beech

Women worshiping are women serving, for worship is service. Frederick Buechner, in his book *Wishful Thinking,* suggests that one way to worship is to do things for God that you need to do. Buechner goes on to say that unless there is an element of joy and foolishness in a worship experience, the time would be better spent doing something else.

Read Mark 14:3-9. As you reflect on this passage, consider Mary's "foolish" act. It was something she needed to do! She came with her alabaster vase filled with pure nard. But she didn't give Jesus a packaged gift and sit back to watch him open it. Instead she broke the vase and poured out its fragrant contents on Jesus' head.

Those in the room reprimanded her harshly. However, Jesus affirmed her, saying that wherever the gospel would be preached, her story would also be told in her memory. What a legacy!

Are you dissatisfied with passive acts of worship? Mary broke her vase and bridged the gulf of silence to the land of deeds. Do you need to break your vase, to sing your song? Maybe you need to create something beautiful for God. Take Mary's step when you join others in the service of worship this week.

Prayer: Holy One, the story of Mary challenges me to active worship. I confess my lack of involvement in too many services of worship. l am often a silent spectator; you call me to participate. It may be costly and even frightening. Prepare me to step into the land of deeds. Amen.

Ingrid Dvirnak
Ontario, Oregon

I Am of God

"You show that you are a letter of Christ, prepared by us, written not with ink but with the Spirit of the living God, not on tablets of stone but on tablets of human hearts."
—2 Corinthians 3:3-4

A year or two ago, I attended the worship service for a friend who was being installed as pastor of a church. One of the guest speakers there encouraged him to remember that "you are your own best thing." Not so long ago, as I was assessing the possibilities for my next career move, the counselor who was helping me said repeatedly, "Now remember, you are enough." And Paul says, "You yourselves are our letter, . . . and you show that you are a letter of Christ . . ." (2 Corinthians 3:2-3).

Having confidence that I am a good person and good at what I do is one thing; thinking of myself as a letter written by the very Spirit of the living God is something else again. Knowing that I am somehow capable of ministering to others is relatively easy; believing that I have qualifications to be a minister of God's new covenant takes more faith. The sheer weight of the responsibility is staggering! Yet this new covenant

3

is one of the Spirit who gives life, encouragement, and power. With this Spirit, we are enough.

As a woman, I often find that following the call of the gospel can be challenging. As a child of God, I am often amazed at how intimidating it can be even to acknowledge that call in the first place. I once attended a meeting of the Society of Friends, and during the silence/response time a woman repeated a quote that her family often used: "Be careful how you live your life; you may be the only Bible some people ever read."

Yes, the responsibility is awesome, but so is the privilege. And the privilege is that we are the letters of the God of love; we are written on human hearts; we are able to touch lives with the message of peace and compassion and mercy. We are of God, and that is enough.

Prayer: Good and gracious God, I am thankful you have chosen me to be your servant in this time and place. I am grateful for the guidance you give me and ask that it may always be accompanied by a sense of your strength. Visit me with power, that I may share the power of your covenant with others. In the name of Jesus I pray. Amen.

Nancy E. Forsstrom
Newton Centre, Massachusetts

True Love

"Look to the LORD and his strength; seek his face always."—Psalm 105:4 (NIV)

This week Tracy was in love with the young male members of a popular rock group whose music and appearance were designed to throw pre-adolescent girls into fits of swooning. She bought all their cassettes, cut out all their photographs from her teen magazines, and shared her heart with all who would listen.

"What's so great about them?" I asked from my unenlightened adult perspective.

"They're so cute!" she gushed.

Frankly, I couldn't see it. But they were the loves of Tracy's twelve-year-old life. She would always love them, she vowed.

"In a few months you'll wonder what you ever saw in them," I countered.

"No! I'll love them forever!"

I held my tongue. Of course she would outgrow them. We all do. No matter how cute and wonderful our infatuations were, there was always another one to sweep us off our feet and be that month's true love.

Sure enough, in a few weeks Tracy was enamored with another singing teen idol. "What happened to your other boys?" I asked.

"Oh, they're stupid. No one likes them anymore," she stated matter-of-factly.

We all feel Tracy's fickle love—and then we grow up. My "Tracy" heart is wiser now. My desire is not for a new infatuation but for a consistent and forever affair.

And this is the treasure of knowing God.

Prayer: God, I don't want to be fickle and trendy when it comes to you. Please keep my heart in true love with you; in Jesus. Amen.

Nancy E. Waugh
Kansas City, Kansas

Is It Right to Love Yourself?

"Thus saith the LORD that created thee . . . and formed thee . . . Fear not: for I have redeemed thee, l have called thee by thy name; thou art mine."—Isaiah 43:1 (KJV)

There are times in our lives when we forget the wonderful fact that God really does love us. Our feelings are often related to the fact that others have given us negative input or some circumstance leaves us with bad feelings about ourselves.

God's Word is filled with positive thoughts that can impact us for good. When you are feeling less than worthy, turn to the Bible and read that God truly loves you and values you as a daughter. Be reminded to "fear not," for you belong to a wise and all-knowing Creator.

Proverbs 23:7 tells us that as we think in our hearts so we are. See yourself as one whom God has created, redeemed, and called by name. This mental picture of yourself will enhance your feelings of self-worth. You can be all that God wants you to be. God's love is not based on your performance. God knows your faults and loves you fully, totally, unconditionally.

Is it right to love yourself? Yes. An unqualified yes. God wants to complete a good work in you. With the psalmist David we can each say, "Surely goodness and mercy shall follow me all the days of my life" (Psalm 23:6).

Prayer: Creator and Redeemer God, help me this day to remember your great love for me and that you continue to complete your good work in me; for Jesus' sake. Amen.

Ruth Housam
Hughesville, Pennsylvania

In God's Image

"So God created human beings, making them to be like himself. He created them male and female, blessed them . . ."—Genesis 1:27-28 (GNB)

When women have asked me to preach on these verses in a church, it is often because they want their congregation to hear about the equality of women and men. One Sunday morning after such a sermon, a few men were irritated and ready for debate.

Off to the side, a lovely woman of seventy years or so waited to speak to me. When she had a chance, she asked, "Do you really believe women are created in God's image as men are?"

"I'm sure of it," I answered. "I wish someone had told me that long ago," she said, looking desperately sad. "I've wasted so many years and so many gifts I've known I had!" We looked at each other with tears in our eyes. She stepped forward and we hugged each other.

This scene needs to be repeated in many of our churches. Archie Bunker's order to his wife, Edith, to "stifle yourself!" in the old TV show "All in the Family" has been the reality for many women at times, even though no deliberate repression is recognized.

When God blessed men and women, God gave the charge to have children and to be good stewards of creation to them both as a shared responsibility. God looked at the creation and was very pleased. God is still pleased today when we use the gifts created in us.

You and I are created in God's image—mind, soul, will, talents. Let's not waste the Lord's creation!

Prayer: Creator God, help us feel the power of your image in us and the joy of knowing we are gifted. Amen.

Janey Smith
Los Angeles, California

A Cleaner Vision

"Eyes are blind to what the mind cannot see."—Sarah Preble

"Do not be conformed to this world, but be transformed by the renewing of your minds, so that you may discern what is the will of God—what is good and acceptable and perfect."
—Romans 12:2

Once a boy named Joey was born to blind parents. He had cerebral palsy and was confined to his home because of his and his parents' limited abilities. As he grew, he began to navigate around the house in a walker. It seemed to his parents that he was of normal intelligence, but clinical tests revealed he was developmentally disabled as well as blind.

When he was five, Joey began attending a school with sighted children. For a while he continued to bump into things and to grope for toys. However, it soon became evident that Joey was not blind but simply had never learned to see. With therapy and interactive play, Joey soon developed normal visual awareness.

Before any art form becomes a reality, the object originates in the artist's mind's eye. Even as she stands in front of a blank canvas, her mind is visualizing line, space, contrast, and mood. The artist first gleans ideas from experience and imagination and the natural world, and then creates her own personal interpretation. For the art to be new and fresh, the artist must follow a new way of "seeing" the familiar.

As with the artist and with Joey, each of us is guided or limited in life by our learned mental pictures of our relationships with persons and things. In order to see ourselves and our global family accurately, we must learn to see as our loving Creator sees.

Prayer: Creator God, enter my mind and create new images so that I might see clearly and correctly. Amen.

Carol S. Willard
Denver, Colorado

The Value of Humor

"A cheerful heart is a good medicine, but a downcast spirit dries up the bones."
—Proverbs 17:22

I have often spoken on the need for humor in our lives. I find that humor helps me to cope with the various difficulties I must face each day. When we take our attention off what is upsetting us and look for the humor, we may see a different perspective of life. Too often the suffering we experience is the result of how we view a situation.

Solomon tells us in Proverbs what good medicine a cheerful heart is. More and more research is showing how humor can even be used to heal physical affliction, "dry bones." When we look for the humor in our lives, it helps to keep us in balance. Humor can offer us a way to avoid a desperate state of mind. Often it is appropriate to laugh, stop worrying about things, and get on with life.

Too often, we are not willing to let go of our difficulties and disappointments, however. Then they become such a burden that their weight keeps us from laughing. In order to live a more abundant life, we need to stop fighting our cir-

13

cumstances. Let them go and accept what God has set before us.

With laughter, we are lifted above our feelings of fear, discouragement, and despair. When we learn to laugh at our setbacks, we no longer feel sorry for ourselves. We feel uplifted, encouraged, and empowered.

Humor is not meant to be an instant cure to all pain or stress. It doesn't necessarily make our pain vanish, but it does give us a new focus. Adding humor to our difficult times can be one of the wisest things we do to help us cope with them.

Take another look at your life, and you will find humor, as I have, in the most unexpected places.

Prayer: God of love and joy, lift our spirits with your Spirit. Show us how to have a cheerful heart in the midst of life's difficulties. Alone we despair, but with you life is abundant. Thank you. Amen.

Terri Simpkins
Seattle, Washington

Contrast and Balance

"I am your God; I will strengthen you, I will help you, I will uphold you . . ."—Isaiah 41:10

I recently completed a photography course that involved working with black-and-white film and manual focusing. This was quite a change for one accustomed to point-and-shoot cameras that automatically produce full-color pictures.

While learning to work in the darkroom, I encountered a most interesting feature of black-and-white photography. Negatives and positives (prints) are both in black and white, of course, with the black areas on the negative white on the print, and vice versa. For the final print to be clear and expressive, with intense blacks and sparkling whites, the negative must be the exact opposite. The contrast is of great importance.

If we envision God as photographer, how do we see the community of believers in the darkroom? We are each created by God. We each have opinions and feelings, and many of us contrast with one another. But in the wondrous creation of God, there is balance. Just as the photographer working in the darkroom looks for the blackest blacks, whitest whites, and most effective shades of grey, we must highlight our

15

contrasts, those differences that make us unique. Then we will be able to highlight the connectedness between us as well.

As women in the church and in the world, identifying our similarities and differences will help us strengthen ourselves. If we were all the same, we would be like a sheet of photographic paper before exposure—undeveloped, without life, and without a message for the world. By developing our contrasts as a part of the total image, we find our completeness in the Creator who made us, upholds us, and strengthens us for our ministries every day.

Prayer: O God, who created both our contrasts and our oneness, we turn to you for wisdom as we seek to highlight the best that each one brings to your work throughout the world. Strengthen and uphold us to be your people; in Jesus' name. Amen.

Kathy Brown
Rochester, New York

Defining God

"I have observed the misery of my people who are in Egypt; I have heard their cry on account of their taskmasters. Indeed, I know their sufferings, and I have come down to deliver them . . ."—Exodus 3:7-8

Today the discussions are frequent about names given to God. Some women reject names for God that imply the masculine. Some men, on the other hand, point out that the Scriptures do not contain female names for God, only motherly or womanly actions and affections.

The contemporary debate might be better focused were we to ask, "What was Jesus' understanding of God?" The Gospels present Jesus in a liberating role, healing and forgiving. Jesus' every action was an expression of God's goodness. Jesus reached out to the poor, to women, and to outcasts; he eliminated barriers that divided groups within society; he embraced the denigrated. Surely the life of Jesus reflected his own understanding and experience of God. To have acted in these ways, Jesus must have understood God to be merciful and compassionate, as caring for the poor and mindful of human suffering.

Jesus' understanding of this kind of God also corresponds with God's self-revelation at the Exodus event. In ancient times, the gods were usually presented as imaging the ways of the powerful in society. The Exodus event presented God in a wholly new way: siding with common people and not with political structures and those who held power.

Jesus' life and work presented God as being on the side of the ordinary poor and oppressed people. Today, unfortunately, as throughout history, people with authority seek to define God for others, often in ways that betray God's character.

Prayer: Most gracious, loving God, show me your face today, that I might know you as you truly are. Help me to acknowledge my own need and poverty of spirit so that I might experience your liberating and healing love and bear witness to others. This I pray through your son Jesus, whom I seek to follow faithfully in word and action. Amen.

Helen Kenik Mainelli
Lombard, Illinois

God the Performer

"...The LORD was with her; and whatever she did, the LORD made it prosper."—Genesis 39:23 (adapted)

A story is told about the great pianist, Ignace Paderewski. A crowd had gathered in the music hall in anticipation of a great performance. A woman who chanced to discover a friend sitting nearby was distracted from her young son, whom she had brought to the performance. When the stage lights went on and the crowd hushed, the woman noticed that her son was missing. Distraught, she looked up and down the aisles, then realized that the child sitting at the piano was her son.

Oblivious to his surroundings, the child began to pick out a tune. The audience gasped when Paderewski stepped out on the stage. He walked toward the piano and gently encouraged the child to continue playing. Paderewski then put his arms around the boy and began to play accompaniment so that the simple tune turned into a masterpiece.

This story speaks to me about the way God works with and through each of us. Our gifts may seem minimal to ourselves, but great things

19

are accomplished when we use our gifts for good. God is always present, always there to sustain and support us. God accomplishes far more through us than any one of us could imagine.

Who is really doing the work? Is it our work or is it God's? For the believing person, it is impossible to see where the human work ends and the work of God begins. It is all the same. Proverbs 16:9 says it well: "The human mind plans the way, but the LORD directs the steps."

Prayer: Creator God, you gave me gifts, and you invite me to do your work. Just as you sent your Son into the world, you send me to be your loving and healing presence wherever I am. My God, I trust that your loving arms enclose me and that you are with me at every moment. Grant me grace, that I may remain faithful to the end; in Jesus' name. Amen.

Helen Kenik Mainelli
Lombard, Illinois

Giving Above and Beyond

" 'Truly I tell you, just as you did not do it to one of the least of these, you did not do it to me.' "—Matthew 25:45

Have you noticed that once you are aware of something, such as a new word, you begin to notice it frequently?

Last spring our adult church school class studied *Rich Christians in an Age of Hunger* by Ron Sider, and we learned that the Bible has much to say about the poor. During the Bible study, references to the rich and the poor constantly popped up—in the prophets, in Psalms, in Proverbs, in Jesus' words and parables.

God's concern for the poor must be your concern, and it must be my concern. Is there a soup kitchen near you? Are you helping in any way? Is your lifestyle simple in this country of excess? Is mine? (I must answer, "Not nearly simple enough.") Are we giving above and beyond our tithe when we are fortunate enough to be able to buy items we want but don't really need? Are our investments oppressing the poor in any way? Are we always concerned for "the least of

21

these"?

I'm just beginning to realize that the poor must always be my concern. I must feed, clothe, visit, give water; I must strive continually to simplify my lifestyle and spend less on myself and my family. I must seek God's will and God's way in this, in all things, as long as I live.

Prayer: O Lord, our Lord, help us to share your concern for the poor. May we give and give until all are filled. Amen.

Ruth Marstaller
Livermore Falls, Maine

Discovering God

*"I found God in myself and I loved Her
I loved Her fiercely."*
—*Ntozake Shange, African American poet*

Recently, while cleaning out some old boxes of college papers and other memorabilia, I found some letters my mother had sent to me years before. She died just a few years ago and, though I feel I am coping with my grief appropriately, I miss her greatly. It was such a pleasant surprise to find the letters and cards I had kept from her over the years. The discovery reminded me of her presence and love for me even though she is no longer here.

Discovering that God is actually a part of us, within us, and loving toward us often comes as a surprise—particularly to women who have been taught that God can be understood only by using male images. To search within oneself and in the Scriptures and to discover that the feminine is as important to God as the masculine will not only inform our theology but also brighten our self-image. To find God in ourselves allows us to celebrate who we are, accept our gifts, and appreciate the life that God has given us. Discover the power of God within you. Find God within yourself and love her.

Prayer: Thank you, God, that you live within me and have called me by name. Amen.

Rosita Mathews
Southampton, Massachusetts

The Value of Our Work

"Therefore, my beloved sisters, be steadfast, immovable, always abounding in the work of the Lord, knowing that in the Lord your labor is not in vain." —1 Corinthians 15:58 (adapted)

Paul concludes his discussion of death and resurrection with a great "therefore." Because the dead rise, because Christ's victory overwhelms death, *therefore* he can categorically affirm the value of a Christian's work.

This is a promise worth holding on to. My ministry of advocacy with the U.S. Congress rarely gives me the chance to say, "I changed a senator's mind" or "We influenced the shape of that law." More often, we wonder why the brick wall never gets lower.

One day I opened the *Washington Post* and read a news story about one political party's reaction to a legislative proposal from a powerful representative of the other party. "Of course we're looking at his proposal," said an unnamed source. "It gives us great partisan leverage." I went nuts. Here we are facing crisis on every side—the economy, drugs, education, health care, housing, racism, you name it—and the movers and shakers are rubbing their hands in glee over a partisan edge.

On days like that, I wonder: Is this work worth the grief? Can we make a difference in the lives of the poor and marginalized?

That's when Paul's longer view provides perspective. I know that what I am doing is in God's will; *therefore,* God will use me. That is enough.

Prayer: God, give me wisdom to discern your hand in the world, and the faith to trust even when I can't see. Amen.

Carol Sutton
Washington, D.C.

Sometimes We Cry

"Likewise the Spirit helps us in our weakness; for we do not know how to pray as we ought, but that very Spirit intercedes with sighs too deep for words. And God, who searches the heart, knows what is the mind of the Spirit, because the Spirit intercedes for the saints according to the will of God."
—*Romans 8:26-27*

Sometimes we cry.

Usually we cry out of our weakness, out of physical or emotional pain. There are times when a thought will bring tears to our eyes; our spirit mourns. There are times when we are ashamed of our tears, thinking that they are evidence of our lack of strength or lack of faith. But we ought not to be ashamed of our tears. Tears are precious, as precious as raindrops upon a parched earth. They are our soul's own cleansing flood that washes away the residue of disappointment and loss and fear, and of anything that wounds us, so that we may be healed.

Rather than feeling ashamed of our tears, we ought to offer our tears to God in the name of Jesus. With every tear that falls, we should quietly say in our hearts, ". . . in the name of Jesus." Jesus is able to take each tear and turn it into a sparkling hope.

And if we cry out of weakness, that is good. It is within weakness that our conscious will cannot contend with the will of God, and the Holy Spirit is able to make intercession for us according to God's will. The apostle Paul reminds us in 2 Corinthians 12:9 that God's power is made perfect in weakness.

When we are in right relationship with God, and when we are praying with correct motives, God hears all our prayers—the spoken prayers and the silent tears. The psalmist writes, "The LORD has heard the sound of my weeping. The LORD has heard my supplication; the LORD accepts my prayer" (Psalm 6:8-9). We have the assurance that when we sow in tears, we will reap in joy.

Prayer: Holy God, thank you for your Spirit, who makes intercession for us. Let your will be done in our lives. Help us to understand that each tear we shed is precious in your sight. We offer them to you in the name of Jesus. Amen.

Valerie Elverton Dixon
Philadelphia, Pennsylvania

My Good Shepherd

"When he saw the crowds, he had compassion for them, because they were harassed and helpless, like sheep without a shepherd."
—*Matthew 9:36*

The biblical writers often compared humans to sheep. If you know very much about sheep, you would not appreciate the comparison. These animals are not very intelligent, and they have no sense of direction. They are afraid because they have no means of protection. Sheep need a leader or they will scatter in all directions. Perhaps people *are* quite similar to sheep!

Jesus refers to himself as the "good shepherd" in John 10:11. He explains that a good shepherd "calls his own sheep by name and leads them out. When he has brought out all his own, he goes ahead of them, and the sheep follow him because they know his voice" (John 10:3-4). The shepherds in Eastern cultures are different from shepherds in Western cultures. For those who have *driven* sheep, it is difficult to imagine a flock of sheep *following* their shepherd. However, the sheep trust and follow the shepherd because he leads them to food and water. Because the shepherd is responsible for every animal, obedience is essential.

The shepherd also knows the individual sheep, calling them by name, putting oil on their cuts and sores. The sheep come to the shepherd for attention. The shepherd rubs the head and ears of the sheep, talking to them as if they were children. The sheep realize that the shepherd cares because of the time he spends with the individual sheep. Likewise, our Good Shepherd wants us to come to him to listen to his encouraging words of love and kindness.

Jesus knows that we humans, mighty as we try to appear, need a Good Shepherd who will lead us over the rough terrain of life. Even before Jesus, the psalmist also knew the human need for a shepherd: "The LORD is my shepherd, I shall not want" (Psalm 23:1). Today, he still restores our souls and leads us in the right paths. When we fall, he picks us up. He calls us by name, loving us always.

Prayer: Good Shepherd, I confess that I often have no sense of direction, that I am helpless and afraid. I ask you to lead me as a shepherd leads the sheep. Thank you for being my shepherd. Amen.

Nita W. Myers
Center, Colorado

Rahab, My Sister

"By faith Rahab the prostitute did not perish . . ."—Hebrews 11:31

Have you noticed that nouns usually accompany certain famous names? Jack the Ripper. Mack the Knife. Elvis the King. Eve the temptress. Rahab the prostitute. Usually the nouns are descriptive; rarely are they complimentary. Such nouns describe only one facet of the person's life; other facets are ignored or forgotten.

We are usually careful when naming a child to avoid names that connote negative thoughts. Rahab's name is unlisted in Dorthea Austin's *Name Book.* Indeed, who would name a girl Rahab, since the noun *harlot* or *prostitute* follows it in the Bible?

We do not know why Rahab was a prostitute. Perhaps she had a financial need. Perhaps she was convinced that she was born to give pleasure to men; tradition tells us she was one of the world's four most baneful women. Would Joshua's two spies have sought pleasure and entertainment from proper women? Of course not, but there in her place of business (built into Jericho's wall) they found comfort and shelter. They never dreamed this "lady of the night"

31

would not only hide them but would lie and help them escape. In exchange, she extracted a promise from them that she and her family would be spared the coming disaster. Beneath that professional facade was a heart in tune with Yahweh. The bargain was struck and a scarlet thread was hung from her window as a reminder of the promise. And it was kept.

Although such a profession as Rahab's evokes disgust, even pity, in us, God used her just as she was. God chose her as an instrument. In Matthew's genealogy, she is listed as the mother of Boaz, who married Ruth, whose blood line flows to Jesus. Isn't it sad that Rahab the prostitute isn't simply remembered as a child of God? Let's not be hasty in accepting derogatory nouns. Rather let's look beyond, see the person, and recognize our relatedness— for, in truth, Rahab is our sister.

Prayer: O Creator of us all, keep me from judging others and open to serving you; in the name of your servant, the Christ. Amen.

Grace T. Lawrence
Lykens, Pennsylvania

Where Did You Go, Lord?

"Why, O LORD, do you stand far off? Why do you hide yourself in times of trouble?"—Psalm 10:1

Sitting alone in the house, surrounded by silence, how I longed for a word from the Lord! I was exhausted, empty, feeling nothing. Color my world grey—dingy grey! The last six months had been the hardest in forty-two years of being a Christian. No matter what I tried, nothing worked. I felt isolated, cut off from friends and family, miserable, and lonely.

Reading my Bible brought no relief or answers. The anger and frustration surging within had turned to desolation and despair. The forgiveness I "willed" brought no peace or satisfaction or reconciliation. My prayers bounced off the ceiling. "Lord, am I losing my mind? Where are you? Why do you stand far off? Why do you hide when I need you the most?" There was no response, no answer. After all these years of trusting and walking with the Lord, always confident in his nearness (Hebrews 13:5), I could no longer feel his presence in any part of my mind, soul, or spirit. I felt dead.

Carol Mayhall, in *Help, Lord, My Whole Life Hurts,* calls these experiences "God's stripping actions"—times when we can't see, hear, or feel God. She suggests they are given to teach us our utter helplessness in controlling life's circumstances, to move us into deeper levels of relationship with our God. The only thing I knew to do was to go through the motions of trusting that Jesus is who he said he was and would do what he said he would do.

Have you ever prayed the Psalms when your world has crumbled? I began praying them daily. Reading them over and over, I asked God for help, hope, and presence. I sang the Scripture to myself as I went for long walks in the sunshine and beauty of God's creation. There was no quick fix; it took months, but I waited on the Lord (Psalm 40:1-3) and in God's time (Ecclesiastes 3:11), I experienced resolution and restoration.

I now believe I needed to come to such a place in my life, to recognize once more my utter helplessness and my inability to change the things I wanted so desperately to change, including myself. I needed to learn in a deeper way that not only is Jesus Christ the rock of my salvation for eternity but also on a daily basis. Because he is, I am. Because he is, I can be whatever he wants me to be!

Prayer: Jesus, you alone are my rock and my salvation. Thank you for reminding me again that you are here in bad times as well as good, in rain and in sunshine. No experience of life is wasted in your economy. You do make all things beautiful in your time. Because I belong to you, isolation is truly impossible. You are always with me, in me—and will always be! Praise you, Jesus! Amen.

Connie Rowe
Sunnyvale, California

Be Joyful

Look to each day with gladness
And expect joy to fill the day.
Trust God to put away sadness
If it comes, unbidden, to your day.
Each day is a fresh page in God's diary.
Yesterday's woes erased.
Seek God for all your inquiries
For in so doing you shall find grace.
Be grateful for the gifts God gives
To each according to need.
Remember our Lord surely lives
And will all of our prayers heed.
So let God's love fill your spirit
As you go about daily task;
God has given us life to inherit,
A kingdom if we but ask!

Jill Haynes Gidge
Nashua, New Hampshire

36

Salvaged by God

"Surely God is my salvation; I will trust, and will not be afraid."—Isaiah 12:2

What is salvation? We think of salvation as the act of saving something from destruction. When we look at the root word, *salvage,* we may think of junk or trash. A salvage yard is a place for wrecked cars that appear to be useless. They are left in a junkyard to rust and rot away. But periodically someone will come along, see something of value in an old automobile, and redeem it, often making it like new again.

I have a son who is a person who can see beauty in what I call junk. He can truly transform junk and make it beautiful. We have a very old pickup truck in our yard that was once in a junkyard. Rick had a vision for that piece of "junk." He rescued the truck from total destruction. After many hours of lovingly pounding out the dents and gently smoothing on a new coat of paint, he created a work of art. I can see the potential and beauty in the truck now.

God sees each of us as a beautiful creation. Too often, however, we do not see the beauty or potential of another individual—or ourselves. Yet God comes to the "junkyard" of our lives, redeems us, and gives us our salvation. Psalm 37:39 says, "The salvation of the righteous comes from the Lord; [God] is their stronghold in time of trouble" (NIV).

When we look for the beauty in our lives as well as in the lives of others, we help to create the people God wants us to be. We reinforce the truth that God does not create junk.

Prayer: God of our salvation, in each of us is a pearl of great price. Thank you for creating us in your image. Help us to see our worth in your eyes. Amen.

Terri Simpkins
Seattle, Washington

Your People Will Be My People

"Where you go, I will go; Where you lodge, I will lodge; your people shall be my people, and your God my God."—Ruth to Naomi, Ruth 1:16

Maria Lugones and Elizabeth Spelman write of developing friendships as the only way to overcome racism. Any other motive, however altruistic, will not work. Their advice to white women is that ". . .from within friendship you may be moved by friendship to undergo the very difficult task of understanding the text of our cultures by understanding our lives in our communities."*

I would underscore three words in their advice: *friendship, difficult,* and *communities.* Rather than beginning on a global scale to try to right the wrongs of racism, Lugones and Spelman suggest that we start with the very personal experience of making friends. This is not easy. It is difficult trying to move beyond the barriers of racism that we have helped to construct. The type of friendship Lugones and Spelman suggest is one that takes seriously the differences

39

of our racial, ethnic, and cultural backgrounds. It takes seriously the differences of family traditions and of differing communities. Only as we understand each other in the communities that give sustenance to our lives do we begin to become friends.

Ruth and Naomi knew something of friendship. They came from different backgrounds, one from Bethlehem and one from Moab. They went through no easy time to become friends and family to each other. They offer us the hope, however, that where you go, I will go—to your home, your turf, where you are yourself. Your people will be my people. We will be one people, one family. Your God will be my God.

Prayer: We pray to you, God of Ruth and Naomi, God of us all, for deeper friendships that bridge the differences that threaten to separate us as women, as your chidren. Amen.

Linda Moody
Oakland, California

*From "Have We Got a Theory for You! Cultural Independence and the Demand for the Women's Voice." Women's Studies International Forum, vol. 6, no. 6, 1983 (Great Britian).

Called to Be a Light

"I have given you as a covenant to the people, a light to the nations, to open the eyes that are blind, to bring out the prisoners from the dungeon . . ."—Isaiah 42:6-7

What are our eyes blinded to that needs to be healed? What imprisons us? What darknesses need to be overcome? What hides our light?

"Physician, heal thyself" is also appropriate to ministers, be they lay or professional, female or male. Are we so focused on privileges and rights (both denied and given) that we are being blinded to the real impetus of our call to be Good News people? Is it possible that the gospel gets buried in the contention between opportunities given and opponents denied? As we reflect the Light by our ministries, it shines more brightly in the world and will not be hidden.

Are we blind to our opponents? God is the One who opens ministry doorways. If we respond faithfully in the small things of life, then God will trust us with the grander arenas.

Does lack of confidence in God's promises imprison us? Are we locked up by fear, ambivalence, and the apprehension of the critical judgment of others? Break out of those dungeons of darkness! Trust in the same miracle that freed Paul and Silas. Bars are removed when the mind and heart are singing praise to God for who God is and what God can do.

Prayer: God, I celebrate who you are and what you have called me to be and do. May nothing stand between us so your true Light can be reflected. Amen.

Anna Belle Poole
Kansas City, Kansas

A Touch of Purpose

*"He said to her, 'Daughter, your faith has made
you well; go in peace, and be healed of your
disease.'"—Mark 5:34*

Linda is a successful partner in a law firm. After working late one night on a case, she was
walking to her car in the company parking lot
when a man jumped her, beat her, and raped
her.

A woman in the crowd is bleeding.

Carol has been married to the same man for
twenty-five years. She loves him. Yet she has to
battle with him every day to gain respect and
recognition as her own person.

A woman in the crowd is bleeding.

Laura is struggling as a single parent because the man she married, the one with whom
she thought she'd spend the rest of her life,
dropped dead of a heart attack and left her with
two small children.

A woman in the crowd is bleeding.

A woman who had been bleeding for twelve
years heard about Jesus. And she came up behind him and touched the hem of his garment,
and immediately her bleeding stopped.

Prayer: Dear Jesus, may we realize that if we reach out to you in faith, with a touch of purpose, you can bring us wholeness. Amen.

Joyce Anderson-Reed
Fairbanks, Alaska

Being the Beloved Is Hard Work

"I compare you, my love, to a mare among Pharaoh's chariots. Your cheeks are comely with ornaments, your neck with strings of jewels."—Song of Solomon 1:9-10

We really don't know why God chooses us. God told the prophet Samuel that the Lord looks on the heart, not on outward appearance (1 Samuel 16:7). God, who looks into the hearts of women, must be pleased with what is visible there. Each of us knows that in some very special way we are the Beloved, just as desired as the Shulamite maiden was.

But being the Beloved is hard work. Note the verses above and consider the life of a mare among Pharaoh's chariots. First, she runs fast! Slow runners don't get chosen. Second, she stands bravely in war. Yes, some of us are old war-horses. Third, she's trained not to rear or bolt. We get battered if we do. Fourth, she's groomed and decorated. Keep those bodies fit! Fifth, she leads the procession. We're certainly on the cutting edge, even though we're often pulling someone else's chariot.

45

So what if we're tired and the job is too hard? We can't get away because "the gifts and the calling of God are irrevocable" (Romans 11:29). And when our bones burn within us, we know there's no quitting. So, we can only fight the good fight, run the race, press on to the goal, rejoice in the Lord . . . and remember, we are the beloved of God.

Prayer: God, grant me courage, strength, wisdom, and beauty. Amen.

Carolyn A. Markham
Anaheim, California

Out of the Circle of Time

"You're arrested!" commanded the officer.

This would be the fourth time. Again, her children would be separated and shuffled to relatives and foster homes. Again, she would sit and wait in a cement cell for a public defender to take up her cause in an overburdened court. Again, the judge, a woman like her (yet so unlike her) would sigh and send her off to wait some more for a drug rehab program to accept her. This time they might not.

Arrested. Time stops. Everything changes.

The birth of my children was like that for me. Pushing and praying, I worked with the waves of pain and power to deliver new life to my trembling arms. The cars go by, people keep appointments and tend to a thousand drudgeries, but for me and mine, time stands still.

The death of a loved one is like that. Arrested, we gather to grieve and let all else gather dust while we attend to the loss and hurt.

It is in this "arrhythmia" that we are most vulnerable—to the Creator, the Christ, the Comforter, one another. As a woman, I ask God to arrest me daily. I ask myself to heed the call of Rumi, the Sufi poet, to "come out of the circle of time, into the circle of love."

In ministry, I watch for others who are arrested by circumstances and ask the Holy Spirit to tune our hearts to refrains of chaos and grace, that growth might take place. For being arrested brings choice: bitterness or betterness. The presence of one who knows Christ and communicates godly acceptance and love during such a time comes away with a greater gift.

Prayer:
"But I trust in you, O LORD,
I say, 'You are my God.'
My times are in your hand; . . .
I had said in my alarm,
'I am driven far from your sight.'
But you heard my supplications
When I cried out to you for help."
—Psalm 31:14,15,22

Sharon Buttry
Swedesburg, Pennsylvania

The Winds of God

"A great windstorm arose . . ."—Mark 4:37

On my carport hangs a lovely, tubular wind chime. It is nice to look at when it is still, but there is no real inspiration from its silence. When there is a breeze, the chimes send forth a gentle or lively sound. People coming to my door stop to listen. Often their faces bear a rapt expression; they feel uplifted. What makes the difference? The wind that blows through the chimes and moves them is the difference.

We cannot see the wind. We feel it. We know it is there. Sometimes this force is gentle; sometimes it is a hurricane. We cannot explain it. There is another invisible force that is even more mysterious—the Spirit of God.

We are like the wind chimes. We can be "good to look at" but no real good to anyone. If God's Spirit dwells within us, however, great things can happen. The Spirit is like the gentle breeze to the chimes. We can be a help or an inspiration to others.

Sometimes God's Spirit gives us a nudge to action. Sometimes we need hurricane-force winds to get us moving. Whatever we feel, let us be aware of the sound of the Spirit of God within us and act. Let us be a sounding chime that brings inspiration and help to others.

Prayer: God, our Creator and Guide, it is so easy to be a lovely chime that does not help anyone. Help us to respond aloud to your Spirit within us so that our daily lives will inspire those around us. Amen.

Margaret B. Bristol,
Ocean Park, Maine

Light and Shadow

"For once you were darkness, but now in the Lord you are light. Live as children of light . . . everything exposed by the light becomes visible, for everything that becomes visible is light."—Ephesians 5:8,13-14

One of my favorite childhood memories is playing in my grandmother's basement. Living next door to her, my brothers and I spent nearly as much time there as we did at home. It was an old-fashioned basement that still had a coal bin, a canning closet, a wringer washing machine, a playroom with a fireplace, and naked light bulbs with old pull cords.

I remember pulling a light cord before going down those spooky stairs. I had memorized where each light cord was, and I would carefully lead the way from one light to the next. Basements are dark and scary places, and the light bulbs cast intriguing shadows on the walls.

The Bible says we are light, and we know that lights cast shadows. We are both light and shadows. We are each made up of many selves. Mostly we try to keep those shadow selves hidden from our own eyes as well as from the eyes of others. But our attempt to do so

51

dims the light that we are to be—the light that transforms. Only when we embrace our shadow selves can we truly praise God with all that is within us. For the love of God in Christ embraces not just the lighter stuff in each of us but also the darker stuff. It is through darkness and shadows that we experience the transforming power of God's light.

Prayer: O Jesus, Light of the World, you know my light side and my dark side. Thank you for loving and accepting all of me. Amen.

Peggy A. Shelton
Warrenville, Illinois

Look at Your Hands

"Whatever your hand finds to do, do with your might."—Ecclesiastes 9:10

Have you ever said, "Nobody will believe I can do that"? We read in Exodus 4 that Moses had been told by God to go tell the people that he had talked with God. Moses was reluctant to do so because he felt the people wouldn't believe him. God told him to look at what he had in his hand. It was only his staff. However, when he obeyed God and threw it on the ground, his staff became a serpent.

Hands can do beautiful things. Take a look at what is in your hand, at what is within your grasp. It's probably not a staff, but you have many abilities you could use for God's purposes. Your skills may be typing, caring for another person, working in the soup kitchen, driving a friend to the doctor, sewing, or folding your hands in prayer for our missionaries and others in need.

Some years ago in the magazine *Guideposts* there appeared the story of a widow who found herself and her family in great financial need. One day she discovered some scraps of cloth and, feeling God was telling her to use the ability she had in her hands, she made beautiful quilts to sell to provide for her family.

Prayer: Our God, consecrate the skills of my hands, the thoughts of my mind, and the use of my time in working with you to make thy world a better place in which to live. Amen.

Betty McClain
St. Petersburg, Florida

Are You the One?

"Are you the one who is to come, or are we to wait for another?"—Matthew 11:3

When John sent his followers to Jesus to ask, "Are you the one?" he really wanted to know, "Have I wasted my time or not? Shall I invest more deeply in you, or shall I give up hope?"

During a visit to Estonia, a newly baptized Christian sister shared with us how difficult it was for her to choose to be baptized. She realized that once she took that step, all of her neighbors would be watching (and listening through paper-thin walls) to see if being a Christian really made a difference in her and in her way of life.

As followers of Christ, we are indeed under scrutiny. Those who have felt rejected by society and the church because of gender, age, race, or ability are looking at us to see if Christ really invites them to be full members of God's community. They are listening to hear whether the language we use includes them. They want to know if we live to bring down walls or build barricades. Spiritually empty friends and materially glutted neighbors are examining our lives for true wealth, hoping that they do not need to look for another to meet their needs.

Society's outcasts are still sending messages from prison, from the streets, from violence-filled homes, asking, "Are you the one who was to come, or should we expect someone else?" Since we believe that Christ is the One who has come for all peoples and all ages, let us live as free, empowered women who embody that truth.

Prayer: All-powerful God, draw us into acts of courage and love, so that our lives say boldly to the watching world that Christ is the One. Amen.

Karen Selig
Manhattan, Kansas

Focusing on Jesus

"So that at the name of Jesus every knee should bend, in heaven and on earth and under the earth, and every tongue should confess that Jesus Christ is Lord ..."—Philippians 2:10-11

I glanced up at the top of my bookcase as I was meditating on the name of Jesus. It jumped out at me, clear as a bell: J-E-S-U-S. Sometimes when I look at the small plaque, I can't see it at all!

Do you know what I'm talking about? I have a plaque with pieces of wood separating the spaces, forming the letters. All too often, by looking at the foreground, all I see is the pattern that the wood makes. And then, just when I'm about to give up, my eye glances over the spaces and I see the letters. The name reveals itself: JE-SUS.

At times we can see Jesus in our life as clear as a bell—perhaps when we are looking into the face of a compassionate friend or cradling a sobbing child. We see Jesus as he lifts up a bent-over woman. We watch him free Martha from her compulsion with duties and tasks. We listen as Jesus teaches Mary. We see Jesus.

But it's too easy to lose our focus. What

seemed clear a moment ago disappears. When we walk down the street, all we see is the dirt on the street person or the badge of authority as the police officer stops our car. We watch churches limiting women's opportunities to use their gifts. We rediscover that a woman's testimony about her abuse is not validated by the court system. We see war and drugs and injustice. We lose sight of Jesus.

Jesus is waiting to be revealed to us. Our job is to focus our sight, so that we see Jesus in the spaces between the wooden pieces of life. Then we will bend our knees in respect and prayer and shout from the housetops that Jesus is Lord!

Prayer: O Jesus, open our eyes so we may see you behind every action, in front of every idea, surrounding our very being. In your holy name we pray. Amen.

Susan S. Maybeck
Pittsford, New York

Dialogue with God

"I will bless the LORD at all times; his praise shall continually be in my mouth."—Psalm 34:1

At daybreak hear my prayer to Thee
Of thanksgiving for a night of rest
And petition for this day's needs;
My path be with Your Spirit blessed.
Midmorning do I also seek You
Discussing barrier and aggravation,
Asking, my rising stress to soothe,
You to turn adversity to celebration.
By noontime do I need Your touch
To strengthen resolve when it starts to fail;
To grant Your grace which means so much
As by frustration I am assailed.
Late afternoon and we meet yet again
In a few quiet moments between chores.
Remember the weary, lost, sick, and then
Confirm in my heart that I am Yours!
Evening draws the day to conclusion
And we talk for the last time this day.
Bless this family and the family of nations.
Help us all to discover Your Way!

Jill Haynes Gidge
Nashua, New Hampshire

God's World

"O LORD, our Sovereign, how majestic is your name in all the earth!"—Psalm 8:1

I get my favorite view of God's majestic world when standing on a high point of an island and seeing the water completely surround that small piece of land. A friend of mine who has always lived on a island delights in standing on a hill on the mainland and being able to see land in every direction. Circumstances and preferences color our outlook, but we all can stand in awe of the majesty of God's world.

As we continue to read Psalm 8, we are told that God has given human beings dominion over God's world and all of its creatures. These are days when we must consider seriously our responsibility to care for this majestic world. Does our sense of stewardship include our responsibility to preserve and renew our earth? What can we do?

Begin at home—live more simply and conserve; recycle; grow your food as you are able; share your love of the earth and what you have of its bounty with others; study to learn about pollution and what can be done to restore the damage already evident; contact legislators, asking them to make the care of the earth a priority issue in politics; and be an example in word and deed to make our world a better place in which to live.

God speaks of love, care, and perfection throughout the created world. Let us accept our responsibility to be good stewards of the dominion God has given us.

Prayer: Creator God, we thank you for the majestic world you have made. Help us to realize what we can do to make it possible for future generations to enjoy the world of majesty we know. Amen.

Lucy P. Thompson
Pembroke, Maine

Miracles Every Day

"Do you not know that you are God's temple and that God's Spirit dwells in you?"
—1 Corinthians 3:16

You have power to perform miracles and change lives! Surprised? Just read 1 Corinthians 12:7-11. Paul expresses Jesus' teaching that even though your faith is as tiny as a mustard seed, lofty mountains are yours to command. Yet we overlook or ignore potential miracles on our doorsteps because we expect a grandstand show. Our sensitivity has been blunted by Hollywood films crammed with action and special effects.

Consider for a moment that you, in some way, affect every single person you pass every day of your life. Whether by a word, a simple deed, or just your presence, both you and the other can be changed forever because of a single encounter.

Consider how much more significant this change can be when Christ is the central focus of your life. A smile may give new hope or comfort. A touch may give renewed courage or strength. A word may bring peace or improved self-esteem. A lifestyle may lend inspiration and guidance. Demeanor or body language may announce acceptance or invite interaction.

Thus, very quietly, are the important miracles of love, healing, witness, and faith accomplished, bringing salvation and joy in Christ into previously bereft lives. In fact, with God's abundant grace and your personal faith, everyone you meet will be able to see Christ looking lovingly back at them!

Prayer: Gracious Spirit, fill my mind and my heart with the power and possibilities to perform miracles of love. Open my spirit to your creative will, and give me the courage to go where you lead; in Jesus' name. Amen.

Jill Haynes Gidge
Nashua, New Hampshire

The Greatest of These

"And now faith, hope and love abide, these three; and the greatest of these is love."
—1 Corinthians 13:13

God's love for us is unending.
God's protection is enfolding.
God's grace is sufficient,
even until the end of time.
Christ expects us to trust him.
Christ wants us to seek him.
Christ encourages us to know him.
Christ guides us toward God with loving
  patience,
tender care, unending
understanding, and awesome tenderness.
Let us listen to God.
Let us hear what God shares.
Let us do as God wills us to do.
God is love.
See God's love and prosper. God's love is
  eternal.
God's love is free!

Prayer: Dear God, enable me to comprehend
your love, accept your grace, and trust you

wholly. I will ever seek your face. You are my all. Thank you for the kind mercy you grant. May I be worthy. Amen.

Gladys Hillman-Jones
Newark, New Jersey

Round Rainbow

"LORD, I know you will never stop being merciful to me. Your love and loyalty will always keep me safe."—Psalm 40:11 (GNB)

Taking the airplane to the church conference center was the most sensible thing to do, I kept telling myself. The journey would take two days by car, we were getting a group rate from the airline, and air travel was statistically safe. Besides, I truly looked forward to viewing the world from thirty thousand feet in the air.

All the positive anticipation and logical reasoning did little to erase the knot in my stomach, however, as the plane began its climb into the skies. Despite the spectacular view of silver rivers, shimmering pools, and the green and brown crazy quilt of farmland, I was quite tense.

Soon the patchwork terrain disappeared and a fluffy layer of white appeared below; above us, a sky of the deepest blue stretched to the horizon. Magnificent as the scene was, my knuckles were turning white with each little lurch or bump.

It was during one of those episodes of turbulence that I first noticed a curious sight outside the small window. On the cloud layer below was the shadow of my airplane, very small but complete in every detail. Completely surrounding the shadow was a rainbow ring, a full spectrum of colors moving along the cloud floor with the plane shadow safely tucked into the middle of it.

Meteorologists have a name for this phenomenon, but for me that round rainbow was a reminder that to believe in God is to believe that we are safely encircled by God's love and promises. We cannot get away from that love, no more than the plane's shadow could escape its position on the clouds.

That wonderful, round rainbow put a smile in my heart that morning and also took away stomach knots and white knuckles. What a visual statement of all-encompassing love!

Prayer:
Lord, help me to sense your ever-present love surrounding me,
supporting me,
protecting me; in Jesus' name. Amen.

Jane M. Grant
Rochester, New York

Christ Has Set Us Free

"For freedom Christ has set us free. Stand firm, therefore, and do not submit again to a yoke of slavery."—Galatians 5:1

The church I grew up in did little to help me gain a sense of self-worth and power. Why was so much emphasis placed on human worthlessness? Why was so little attention given to proclaiming God's freeing love? The Sunday the Good News was preached must have been the one I missed. Repeatedly, I heard the "you are a worthless sinner" message and missed the "you are loved and empowered by God" message.

I heard preachers declare as biblical truth that women are inferior beings and cursed as daughters of Eve. It didn't seem fair to me and inwardly, even as a child, I began to question. Of course I did not voice my questions; questioning was not encouraged, especially by women and children. In fact, it was rare for a woman to speak at all in that church, although they taught children's classes in the Sunday school.

Eventually, I found places—college, seminary, feminist groups, and so on—where questions could be asked. I found Christians who had experienced God's empowering love and could share their own questions and insights. I found the Bible speaking to me in a new way, now freed of the narrow restraints that had blocked its messages of affirmation and hope.

Today I rejoice in a growing awareness of God's transforming love. The messages that fostered a spirit of worthlessness and powerlessness were false teachings. It is good to know that God's message in the Bible and in Christ is one that frees and empowers us.

Prayer: Loving God, help us to hear and respond to your call to freedom. Help us to resist ideas and practices that enslave us as women and keep us from accepting your gifts of love and power and self-determination. Amen.

Verge Gillespie
Chester Springs, Pennsylvania

Do Not Be Afraid

"They saw Jesus walking on the sea and com-
ing near the boat, and they were terrified. But
he said to them, 'It is I; do not be afraid.'"
—*John 6:19-20*

Have you ever wondered why the disciples
were afraid when they saw Jesus coming toward them on the water? He was their friend
and their teacher, and they had seen him perform many miracles. But when they saw him
walking toward them across the water, they
cried out in fear.

Maybe they were afraid because they recognized the extraordinary power of Jesus and
didn't know what he might expect of them.

That's just the point at which most of us are
afraid in our contact with Jesus. When Jesus
comes walking toward us on the sea of our troubled lives, we get a bit nervous. There he is,
with the waves thrashing around him, striding
purposefully toward us, his eyes looking deep
within our souls, and he expects us to be obedi-
ent to him even as the waves obey him. Our
hearts race, and we are afraid.

What if he should ask us to get out of our
comfortable boats and walk in the stormy sea

with him, risking all that is familiar and safe? Supposing he should say to us, "I have some things I want you to do that you have never done before," or "I want you to try a new approach to an old task, to do something risky that is not guaranteed to succeed."

Jesus spoke to the disciples and calmed their fears. He said, "It is I. Don't be afraid." Fear has the power to immobilize us, to paralyze us. But Jesus comes to us across the stormy seas of our lives and invites us to overcome our fear and walk with him in power.

Prayer: O Christ, our Friend and Redeemer, help us to use the power you have given us to overcome our fears and leave our safe, comfortable ways to walk boldly the new paths in our stormy seas with you. Amen.

Rachel Gillespie Lee
Haddonfield, New Jersey

Thirsting for God

"O God, you are my God, I seek you,
my soul thirsts for you;
my flesh faints for you,
as in a dry land where there is no water."
—Psalm 63:1

Picture yourself in the desert with the sun beating down on you. Sweat pours off your body. Your lips are parched, your throat is dry, and your entire body is weak because of the lack of water. Then you see a pool of water, and there's hope. As you run toward the water, the closer you get to it the farther away it seems to be. You soon discover it's only a mirage. Wandering in the desert wilderness, you die of thirst.

As children of God, we should always seek God, thirst for God. The more we seek, the more God quenches our thirst. Even in the dry places in which we find ourselves, we should yet long for God. As Christians, we know the water that God gives us *will* continue to spring up daily. We will not die of thirst.

In the work that God has called each of us to do, we must seek God and stay full of the water, which is the Spirit of God. In Christ we have living water and everlasting life.

Prayer: Dear Lord, thank you for reminding us that you are always there for us, ready to quench our thirst. What joy we receive when we commune with you! Help us to lean and depend on you like never before. Continue to empty us out, and fill us up daily with good things. We thank and praise you. Amen.

Linda F. Long
Yorba Linda, California

Regarding Superstitions

" 'If I but touch his clothes, I will be made well.' "—Mark 5:28

What must the woman in this story have felt? Bleeding for twelve long years, searching everywhere for a cure, trying every treatment imaginable, using all of her meager financial resources. Isolation? Loneliness? Fear? Frustration? Rejection? Desperation? A glimmer of hope? Could this Rabbi/Healer/Teacher help? Would it hurt to try?

Unclean, unwanted, unapproachable, ostracized—her only hope for healing was Jesus, and he was surrounded by loud throngs of people, clamoring for his attention. Perhaps if I can get close enough to touch just his clothes, I will be healed and he will never know the difference, she thought.

But he did know—immediately. "Who touched me?" His eyes pierced through the crowd, searching for the one who sought salvation. Their eyes locked, and the woman fell at his feet, confessing everything in gratitude and thanksgiving for her liberation. Jesus' benediction—"Go in peace and be healed of your disease" (Mark 5:34)—confirmed her knowledge that she had been made whole and that the source of her cure was not magical clothing but rather God's power at work through Jesus the Healer.

Can I continue to look for answers in superstitions and half-truths? Do I dare to approach Jesus with my fears and insecurities? How much longer will my own sense of isolation and rejection keep me from the Source of healing and wholeness, of salvation?

Prayer: Gracious and Loving God, I want to know your wholeness, your peace, your salvation in the midst of the brokenness and shattered dreams of my life. In thanksgiving and gratitude, I lay these now at your feet, ready to rise as a new woman, whole and free. Amen.

Soozi Ford
Casper, Wyoming

Access to Grace

"Therefore, since we are justified by faith, we have peace with God through our Lord Jesus Christ, through whom we have obtained access to this grace in which we stand . . ."
—*Romans 5:1-2*

Prior to earning the status of Girl Scout, I was a Brownie— which in my day meant wearing a brown beanie and holding up two fingers instead of three. It also meant wearing an official uniform to meetings.

I didn't have a uniform. I'm not sure why I didn't have one. Perhaps my parents didn't have the means or the energy to get me one. Whatever the reason, I ended up being the only imp without the proper browns.

There was a ceremony in which we Brownies each recited magical words and received a special pin. As we waited off-stage, a troop leader came in and said she had a new uniform for a Brownie named Laura. It was too good to be true! As I stood speechless, another Laura responded, somewhat confused, and replaced her old uniform with the new one. Later, I learned that the new uniform *was* for me; my mother had been trying to surprise me.

I still struggle with believing I am worthy of such surprises, such grace—even when there is no mistaking that God calls me by name. We were taught as little girls that we are unworthy of life's gifts, and we easily translate that into a theological conclusion that prevents us from accepting salvation and inclusion.

But now I know that feeling unworthy is my struggle, my sin, as I believe it is for many women. We do not wrestle with pride or self-love but with the lack of it. For us, the challenge of personal spirituality is to be open to hearing God call our names, and then to be able to respond, "Here am I; I am ready to receive your grace."

Prayer: God, forgive me my sin. Thank you for continuing to give me access to your grace. I accept it; in Jesus' name. Amen.

Laura Alden
Elverson, Pennsylvania

Commitment Is . . .

"Then Mary said, 'Here am I, the servant of the Lord; let it be with me according to your word.'"—Luke 1:38

A young woman and the man who was to become her husband were called by God to an "impossible," illogical, incomprehensible commitment. They were called to participate in God's ultimate commitment to redeem creation.

During the Advent season we are called to reflect upon the gift of God's Son and upon our response to that gift. The responses of Mary and Joseph were probably not unlike those that we experience.

So often God chooses to be revealed to us in the midst of the ordinary (Mary, in her home; Joseph, as he struggled with decisions). Neither Mary nor Joseph could have anticipated being chosen to participate in the fulfillment of God's promise to Israel.

Sometimes we are requested to do that which seems impossible within ourselves to accomplish (Mary, a virgin; Joseph, a righteous and compassionate man). There seems to be no logical response to God's messenger. Yet, while they were not given the details they may have wanted, they were given the information they needed.

God works through people to fulfill promises. The promise of the Messiah could not have been fulfilled without the commitment of Mary and Joseph. Mary's response, "Here am I, the servant of the Lord; let it be with me according to your word" (Luke 1:38) sums up the commitment that both she and Joseph demonstrated in the days that followed.

Likewise, our commitment is demonstrated through our actions.

Prayer: Here I am, Lord. Show me what you want me to do. Because of your gift of love, Jesus Christ, I am willing. Amen.

Louise B. Barger
Valley Forge, Pennsylvania

A Song for My Mother

"I am reminded of your sincere faith, a faith that lived first in your grandmother Lois and in your mother Eunice and now, I am sure, lives in you."—2 Timothy 1:5

When my mother was pregnant with me, she watched the assassination of President John F. Kennedy on TV. My unborn child and I watched the Persian Gulf War together.

The patterns repeat themselves, as do the cycles of life. In the midst of a frightened, angry world, I thought, "What lullaby should I sing to comfort my child?" Not surprisingly, the song my mother sang to me, that her mother had sung to her, drifted across the decades.

"Jesus loves me, this I know. For the Bible tells me so. Little ones to him belong. They are weak but he is strong. Yes, Jesus loves me. Yes, Jesus loves me. Yes, Jesus loves me. The Bible tells me so."

I placed my hands on my stomach and sang the lullaby to my unborn child. Another generation coming into the world. An old song, yet a new song, to sing glory to God. I wonder if my child will change the world. All mothers think that—including Mary of Nazareth looking at her newborn son in the manger. Children do grow up and change the world, especially children who grow up following where the baby Jesus leads them.

The patterns of faith continue. Throw a pebble in the pond, and watch the ripples expand. Our circle begins with God. It ripples out through Adam and Eve . . . and down through the myriad of years to my grandmother Britomarte, to my mother Mary, to me, to my unborn child. A song from one mother to the next.

Prayer: God of our mothers, may we never hesitate to sing a "Jesus Loves Me" song to our children, the next generation. Amen.

Joyce Anderson-Reed
Fairbanks, Alaska

What Christmas Means to Me

"To you is born this day in the city of David a savior, who is the Messiah, the Lord."—Luke 2:11

One Christmas, a young teacher and I were visiting over a cup of coffee in my classroom. Suddenly she said, "You know what I like best about Christmas—'Tom and Jerrys'!"

I knew then that I needed to share with her and all who came into my classroom the true meaning of Christmas. So I prepared a bulletin board with the following poem as the focal point, and I prayed that God would use it to cause all who saw it to understand what we are celebrating at Christmas.

Christmas to some means presents,
To others a Christmas tree,
To some it may mean a party:
That's not what it means to me.
To some it may mean a brand new dress,
Or candy and cake and tea,
To some it may mean another good time;
That's not what it means to me.
On Christmas we do receive presents,

We have a Christmas tree, too,
But to me it means the Christ Child's birth;
Is that what it means to you?
—Anonymous

Prayer: Dear Lord, help us not to get so caught up in our material celebration of Christmas that we lose the great blessing of your love in the gift of your Son to us. Amen.

Amy Barber
Owanka, South Dakota

Accepted and Chosen by God

"The angel said to her, 'Do not be afraid, Mary, for you have found favor with God.'"—Luke 1:30

"You have found favor with God." These words came to an ordinary teenage girl living with her parents. She wasn't powerful or famous. Her fiancé was only a poor carpenter in a little, obscure village called Nazareth. She had no reason to believe that she was known and chosen by God for a special work in the world. It troubled and perplexed her just to hear the words said. Yet somehow, she came to accept the truth in the message of the angel, "Mary, you have found favor with God."

It is the same statement that many modern women find impossible to believe. I myself find it hard to accept when the Spirit whispers, "Karen, you have found favor with God." In a world that so often conspires to disempower and devalue women, it's not easy to trust that we have God's approval and love. But it's true! God has seen you, known you, and accepted you. Whatever your background, age, race, or place in society, you have found favor with God. The most impossible happening—that God has noticed and regarded you as an individual—has come true.

Prayer: Most Holy God, teach me that in you, nothing is impossible. Help me to recognize and affirm the favor of your love in my life. Amen.

Karen Selig
Manhattan, Kansas

Reflections on a New Year

"LORD, you have been our dwelling place in all generations. . . . from everlasting to everlasting you are God. . . . For a thousand years in your sight are like yesterday when it is past . . ."
—Psalm 90:1-2,4

"Yet you do not even know what tomorrow will bring. What is your life? For you are a mist that appears for a little while and then vanishes."—James 4:14

In the midst of winter, dead leaves, frozen ponds . . . a new year begins. At the stroke of midnight, all becomes new! Or does it? Of course not! Only the calendar is new, and we become aware once again that time marches on.

Remember how long a year seemed to be when you were a small child? Even a week seemed an eternity. This new year, take time to experience a child's perspective on time. What's it like to always wait for someone else? What would it be like not to know how long an hour is, or a day? What is it like to never know what comes next? Perhaps a child's perspective is closer to the perspective God wants us to have on eternity. Come to God as child, and let God surprise you this coming year.

Prayer: Dear God, open our hearts to the wonder of creation, even in the midst of winter. Surprise us with each new day and each new year. Let this day be filled with your love. Amen

Peggy A. Shelton
Warrenville, Illinois

Listening for God

"9-1-1. That's my prayer life. I don't have time for any more."

Paul Tournier, the Swiss psychiatrist, tells a story about a distinguished woman who was talking to a group of people in her living room. She was deploring the fact that she had never been touched by God's grace. "How is one to believe that God exists?" she asked. If God existed, would she not have had some answer from God in her twenty-five years of making requests?

"Pardon, Madame," remarked one of her guests, "but did you ever leave time for God to get a word in?"

Is it possible that we fail to listen to God's answers to us? Just sit and listen. It's not one more "thing" to be done. Being in God's presence, sitting and listening, enables us to complete our other tasks refreshed. When we listen to the voice at our center, we understand what Paul wrote to the Galatians: "It is no longer I who live, but Christ who lives in me" (Gal. 2:20).

Prayer: Please, God, help me find spaces in my busy day to listen to you. May I become more comfortable with the silences of life. Amen.

Jane D. Wallbrown
Essex Junction, Vermont

Life's In-between Stages

"Life is filled with swift transitions" are the words of the hymn writer who reminds us of the changing world in which we live and the unchanging nature of God. William Bridges, author of *Transitions,* cites that there are usually three phases that depict the transitions in our lives: leaving the old, embracing the new, and the unpleasant "in-between stage." The in-between stage is a state of limbo, or an entrance into one of the great intersections of life with uncertainty about which way to go.

The apostle Paul was at one of life's crossroads immediately after his Damascus Road experience. "For three days he was without sight, and neither ate nor drank" (Acts 9:9). During this "in-between stage," he is likely to have spent time reflecting on his old life and contemplating his new life. Imagine sitting in a dark, lonely room as a guest of a person who was your enemy. In that room Paul probably reflected on the confrontation with sin and salvation he had just had. No doubt, his own personal sins seemed as large as life. Physically, Paul was still, but spiritually Paul advanced. Paul's understanding of the Scriptures taught him that his experience was beyond human understanding, so he turned to Christ.

Standing in between the old and the new is difficult because we are not always thrilled about where we have been, and we certainly do not know where we are going. This was true in the case of Paul. Paul could not have known that God was preparing him for stonings, rejection, beatings, and prison bars—and for the task of writing a large portion of the New Testament.

During our "in-between stages," God is also preparing us for unknown challenges, victories, and defeats. We must learn to cope with the ambiguity that is present during life's transitions because these may be periods of spiritual renewal. Though we may seem in these days, weeks, and sometimes years to be wandering in the wilderness, God will restore our sight during those times, give us new direction, and guide us into all truth.

Prayer: God of change and new life, give me patience and hope during my time of transition. Help me to see the direction you want me to go, and give me the courage and strength to proceed. Amen.

Dolores E. McCabe
St. Davids, Pennsylvania

Seeds of Life

"If our God has given to earth the art to nestle seed whilst the seed is seemingly dead, why shall [God] not give to the heart of [people] to breathe life into another heart, even a heart seemingly dead?"—Kahlil Gibran

When we turn on our television or read the newspaper, the news is generally negative and disheartening. In many walks of life, fellow humans seem to hold little, if any, regard for the personhood of others. Crime and unemployment seem to be on the rise, while educational opportunities and human development programs receive less and less attention.

Let us not become discouraged, though, for the love of Christ is powerful enough to reach through us to touch the seemingly dead heart of another. We must allow ourselves to be the vehicles of love that transport life.

Prayer: Dear God, please use me as a seed of your love so that others might learn of you and have life through Jesus Christ. Amen.

Gladys Hillman-Jones
Newark, New Jersey

Perfect Creations

"God saw everything that he had made, and indeed, it was very good."—Genesis 1:31

At the first sign of spring, we once again begin to work on making our bodies into fit specimens that any fitness guru would be thrilled to have. We huff and puff and sweat, trying to coax our bodies into something other than what they have been during the winter months. Inspired by signs of new life, and resurrection, we hope to be transformed into an image that may suit Madison Avenue, but in reality may be quite different from the women God created and intended us to be.

For women in this country, one of the difficult lessons to learn is appreciating physical differences. Because one physical type is held up as the ideal of female beauty, we may think less of ourselves if we do not measure up to that model. The joy of being created in the image of God is knowing that God has more than one standard of beauty. God has a variety of images of beauty that includes all ages, abilities, and racial and ethnic characteristics.

We all want to look and feel the best that we can, and we should practice good stewardship by caring for our physical, emotional, and spiritual needs. But there is a difference between taking care of ourselves physically and remaking what God has created. We are perfectly made in the image of God. During this time of spring, let us remember to appreciate the beauty of creation, which includes our bodies.

Prayer: Holy Creator, help me to know that I am wonderfully made in your perfect image. Amen.

Patricia L. Hunter
Seattle, Washington

The Gift of Sexuality

"A garden locked is my sister, my bride,
a garden locked, a fountain sealed.
Your channel is an orchard of pomegranates
with all choicest fruits, henna with nard,
nard and saffron, calamus and cinnamon,
with all trees of frankincense,
myrrh and aloes, with all chief spices—
a garden fountain, a well of living water,
and flowing streams from Lebanon."
—*Song of Solomon 4:12-15*

Unclean! Unclean! What a terrible label to bear in ancient times! Cultic laws traced the source of women's uncleanliness to our sexuality. The functions of our bodies that enable us to bring forth new life—menstruation and childbirth—were believed to pollute us, to separate us from the community of the righteous, to require ritual cleansing.

Unclean! Unclean! The echo of ancient voices is still with us when we dishonor our female bodies and our sexuality as ugly or dirty or a hindrance to spirituality. Solomon's song lifts up another image: women's sexual being as an Eden-like garden, a source of nourishment and abundance, even of living water—an image later

94

used by Jesus (John 4:10) to refer to the gift of eternal life.

Prayer: Giver of eternal life, give us the grace to unlock the gardens of our bodies to be the sources of physical and spiritual life and nourishment that you meant them to be. Amen.

Betsy Sowers
Leominster, Massachusetts

To See Thee More Clearly

"Day by day,
Dear Lord, of these three things I pray:
To see thee more clearly
Love thee more dearly
Follow thee more nearly
Day by day.
Amen."
—St. Richard of Chichester (1197-1253)

Jesus brought a new vision! The world had never seen God so clearly before! Jesus was born, and God came to earth. Jesus saw things differently. He recognized the worth of children, and he knew the value of women. He considered all of life to be good. "Consider the lilies of the field, how they grow" (Matthew 6:28).

From the Gospel writings we see who Jesus is. His teachings, parables, and miracles all serve to help us to "see thee more clearly." We are challenged by these words—to see more clearly the One who has come on our behalf to reconcile us to God, who loves us with an unconditional love. We wish to see God more clearly, love God more dearly, to follow God more nearly

. . . and it is Jesus who gives us the grace and strength to do just that.

The process by which we see, love, and follow is both slow and painful, quick and joyous. It is the process of a lifetime, and a process that, as Richard of Chichester once proclaimed, can only be pursued "day by day." May each of us see, love, and follow with clarity of vision.

Prayer: Day by day, dear Lord, of thee three things I pray: to see thee more clearly, love thee more dearly, follow thee more nearly, day by day. Amen.

Linda Estabrook Bonn
Pasadena, California

The Extravagant Gift

"While he was in Bethany, reclining at the table in the home of a man known as Simon the Leper, a woman came with an alabaster jar of very expensive perfume, made of pure nard. She broke the jar and poured the perfume on his head."—Mark 14:3 (NIV)

Extravagance is not a word we often associate with the gospel. And yet in this story Jesus commends this unknown woman for her extravagant giving. Brought up in a world that advocates that giving should be steady and measured, not impulsive, I wondered, What made her gift acceptable to Jesus?'

Perhaps her gift was accepted because the motive of her giving was love. Jesus' disciples were caught up with his political power. Often they asked, "What's in this for me?" "Who will be the greatest?" "Where will I sit in the kingdom of God?" The woman anointed Jesus not as a power play, not to be manipulative, not for her own personal gain or recognition, but out of love.

She was not afraid to give her valuable possession to honor Jesus. And by doing so, she was able to serve Jesus in a way that none of her male counterparts seemed able to comprehend: she served Jesus extravagantly, recognizing that he had come to do the same for her. Extravagant giving. Extravagant service. Extravagant love.

This unknown woman presents us with a challenge. Where is God asking us to give extravagantly in our Christian lives? Where do we need to let go, beyond the boundaries, beyond the expected, to further the gospel of Jesus Christ?

Prayer: Dear God, may the story of this woman challenge us to think about giving—extravagantly; in the name of Jesus. Amen.

Joyce Anderson-Reed
Fairbanks, Alaska

Rejoice!

"Rejoice, rejoice ... Shout for joy!"—Zechariah 9:9 (GNB)

When our daughter started school, it was with a shout of joy and much rejoicing. When my husband came home from Vietnam with his limbs intact, there were shouts of joy and rejoicing. When the presents were opened on those days of special occasions, joyous shouts, merriment, and rejoicing took place.

With each of these events, we had a time of preparation. Special clothes were purchased, appointments were made, special modes of transportation were sought, even our attitudes were transformed; we were all rejoicing and shouting. We were preparing to receive a blessing. A prayer had been answered, and there was the shout of joy and the moment to rejoice.

Zechariah brings this message into focus for us. The future for the people of Israel seemed bleak. They had gone through the wilderness journey—and up and down with their emotions. They, too, had had moments of joy and thoughts of rejoicing and merriment. Zechariah brings hope to the people in the middle of his prophetic message—hope that there would be a king. The king would not arrive with the lavish entourage that usually accompanies such a regal, royal visitor to the city. This king would arrive, humbly, on a donkey colt. This king would ride on the beast of burden, triumphantly. And triumphant, the king did ride for the people of Jerusalem and Judah.

Jesus the Christ will ride symbolically through our hearts this season, reminding us that we are to rejoice and shout with joy, for our king is coming. Rejoice, rejoice! Shout for joy!

Prayer: Dear Heavenly Parent, Thank you for the joy in our hearts. Let us rejoice and shout with joy, "Our king is coming! Our king is coming!" Amen.

Bonita A. Kitt
Oakland, California

What about Fasting?

"Share your food with the hungry. . . . Give clothes to those who have nothing to wear."
—Isaiah 58:7 (GNB)

Those of us who grew up in a time when Protestants did not consider fasting important have questioned the reason or requirement for such an act. Yes, fasting would be good for a person. Most could benefit from giving up desserts and losing a few pounds. But how would that serve the Lord or help our spiritual progress?

Perhaps "giving up" some things with a promise to say a prayer instead of indulging a craving would help our individual prayer lives for a while. But, when we read Isaiah's account of what true fasting should be, we find unmistakable advice: We should fast not to help ourselves but to be made aware of others. There are people in need all around us.

Feed the hungry. Form a group to collect money on a regular basis and buy food in quantity for a hunger distribution center near you—or start one if there is not one now. Offer to help feed those who come to a center for a meal. Visit a shelter for homeless or battered women and children. Offer your help in job hunting, tutoring, babysitting, fund-raising—wherever you are needed. Do this in the name of Jesus the Savior, and you have truly fasted for the Lord.

Prayer: Lord, all that I am, and all that I hope to be, I have received from you. Bless and strengthen me as I fast for you by giving to others. Amen.

Muriel B. Bristol
Cleveland, Ohio

Drinking from the Rock

" 'I will never leave you or forsake you.' "
—Hebrews 13:5

Both biblical history and Jewish tradition advise us that when the children of Israel were in the wilderness, God led them through their entire pilgrimage. During the day God led them by a cloud; at night God led them by a pillar of fire. They were given manna to eat and water that flowed from a rock. In this dispensation of types and shadows, the rock that followed them was Christ (1 Corinthians 10:4).

In spite of divine guidance, divine supply, and divine presence, many of them fell into temptation and perished in the wilderness. The apostle Paul says, "These things happened to them to serve as an example, and they were written down to instruct us" (1 Corinthians 10:11). The word of instruction comes to us in a reminder that while we are Christians (those who drink from the rock), we are subject to temptations that lead to falling even though the Lord is with us. Those of us who think we are strong in the Lord are particularly susceptible because we sometimes think we've "arrived." But again the apostle warns us, "So if you think you are standing, watch out that you do not fall" (1 Corinthians 10:12).

Now that we have the risen Christ living in us by his Spirit, utter dependence upon him and drinking in his presence through prayer, Christian meditation, and scriptural reflection will assure that his strength is made perfect in our weakness. We have no need to make pilgrimages to sacred wells; the rock is following us. I can still hear him say, "I will never leave you or forsake you."

Prayer: Dear Lord, help me to sense your continuing presence in my life, today and everyday, as my source of strength and my soul's joy. Amen.

M. Frances Manning
New York, New York

Do We Remember?

"I gave my back to those who struck me, and my cheeks to those who pulled out the beard; I did not hide my face from insult and spitting."—Isaiah 50:6

As we prepare for this Easter season, let us reflect on Isaiah 40:3-9 and ask, "Do we remember?"

That the beatings, the name calling,

The hatred in the eyes of the people,

The pain of the bruises, the pain of not
   understanding what his accomplishments meant,

The unwelcomeness of the community Jesus was nurtured in, did not accept him,

The spit that was heaved onto his body

The humiliation of having hair pulled from his beard,

Do we remember? Remember why it was done?

It was done so that you and I would be able to
   have a right to the Tree of Life,

It was unmerited grace and mercy.

That is why we do remember.

Prayer: Lord Jesus, we thank you for helping us

to remember your pain for us. May we acknowledge this unmerited grace and mercy. Amen.

Bonita A. Kitt
Alameda, California

True Rest

"Come to me, all you that are weary and are carrying heavy burdens, and I will give you rest."—Matthew 11:28

True rest is a gracious gift that comes to us when we take upon ourselves God's way of life—God's "yoke"—and enter into a deep, abiding relationship with God. This relationship forms a center for our lives from which we can move out to personal fulfillment and service to others. It also serves as a place of refuge and rest in which to be renewed amidst the weariness and burdensomeness of life.

I caught a glimpse of the transforming power of such companionship as I observed the interaction between two-year-old Zach and his mother at our church camp. He would often wander off to play a game, explore some new discovery, or gather seashells with a teenage friend. But every so often, he would experience overload, overwhelmed by unfamiliar people, surroundings, and routines. Then he would run for his mother, stretch his little arms up in the air, and cry to be held.

I would watch Zach rest on his mother's lap, enveloped by loving arms, sometimes chattering animatedly, sometimes sitting motionless in exhausted silence, content to just be close to her.

Soon he would be off again to a new adventure, having found in that brief time out what he needed to keep going. In our world of burnout, stress-out, and give-out, our heavenly Parent invites us to come, to be close, to find rest for our lives.

Prayer: Dear God, help me to deepen my relationship with you. When life overwhelms me, help me to take a time out with you so that I may find the security, serenity, and strength I need to cope and to become the person you created me to be; in Jesus. Amen.

Cheryl A. Brown
Bakersfield, California

Jesus Wants Us to Live

"Jesus said to her, 'I am the resurrection and the life. Those who believe in me, even though they die, will live.'"—John 11:25

Jesus can give us life that death can't erase. He has the power to do that no matter what the obstacles are that bind us. Jesus raised Lazarus from the dead to help us understand the power of God, to help us see that God has control over every kind of death. When Jesus stepped up to the tomb and cried out, "Lazarus, come forth!" Lazarus obeyed.

The voice of Jesus echoes down through the centuries. He cries out again and again, to you and to me: "Come forth from the tombs that imprison you. Come forth to new life, real life!" Jesus' voice of authority demands that we come forth from the bondage that shackles us with its death hold.

The emphasis is on life, not just the resurrection. Who wants to be resurrected to the same old meaningless existence? It's life that people want! This miracle is a sign that Jesus can renew our dead lives.

Sometimes we are bound by gender restrictions. For many years I was dead to the call to do certain types of ministry because I had grown up believing that women were not supposed to do those things. But one day I heard Jesus' authoritative voice command me to come forth, to throw off the bindings that kept me as silent as the dead Lazarus.

Jesus continues to call us out of our tombs—tombs of sin and doubt, tombs of materialism, sexism, and ageism. Without regard to gender, he calls us to use our gifts as God and the Holy Spirit direct.

Prayer: Loving Creator, give us the ability to come forth from the tombs that imprison us, and help us to be all that you intend us to be. Amen.

Rachel Gillespie Lee
Westmont, New Jersey

111

Soaring

"One can never consent to creep when one feels an impulse to soar."—Helen Keller

Still we soar . . .
    though our wings have long since dried,
    though our shells have decayed, leaving no
trace
        of the place they
                fell.
    Not with the early enthusiasm of swiftly beat-
ing flutters,
    nor with excited utterances that make our
flight an exclamation mark,
    But with a gentle confidence, we wing our
way aloft . . .
    Catching a ride on the Breath that is God's
ever-presence to us,
    And we soar—hour after hour, day by day,
year following year,
    Riding the waves and crests of life on wings
propelled by love,
    Hearts caught up in the grace of the One who
broke the walls of our cocoons
        and set us free to new life with the words,
                        "Follow me."

Prayer: To you, O Ever-Present One, do we lift up our hearts. Keep them aloft this day with the joyous knowledge of your grace alive in us. Amen.

Karen Selig
Manhattan, Kansas

Laboring Toward New Life

"We know that the whole creation has been groaning in labor pains until now . . ."
—Romans 8:22

If you have ever been around someone giving birth, you know about labor. Now this may sound remarkably naïve, but it took me until my third pregnancy to believe in the pains of labor. The first time I was convinced that if you just breathed right, there would be no pain. The second time I thought that subsequent labors would be different. By the third time, I knew better; I knew that labor always involves pain. The fourth and fifth times simply confirmed it.

The pain of labor, however, takes its meaning from the anticipated outcome. During my first labor I had a companion in pain, a hospital roommate whose baby had died in the womb. While we both experienced the same process, I expected at the end a baby to cradle in my arms, and she knew that her arms would be empty. The anticipated outcome made the difference.

The labor pains of creation will produce the outcome of a world that truly is very good. Jesus

Christ is the yes and amen to all God's promises inherent in creation that this goodness shall be so. Giving birth to new life is hard work. Yet Jesus Christ prepares us by guaranteeing the outcome and by breathing the breath of the Spirit into our beings. When life seems too painful and going nowhere, take heart. God, who is closer to you than your own breath, labors with you, and a new creation is being born.

Prayer: O God, as you have borne us and bear with us, labor over us still until all things are made new. Amen.

Kate Penfield
Providence, Rhode Island

Mothers and Daughters

"Love does not resolve every conflict; it accepts conflict as the arena in which the work of love is to be done."—Daniel Day Williams

When daughters become adults, we and our mothers sometimes have trouble forging an appropriate relationship. Are we now peers? Can a daughter still say, "Mom, take care of me," even after she has children of her own? Can a mother expect her daughter to parent her when she feels vulnerable?

We can answer yes to all of those questions. A mother-daughter relationship can't remain static when each woman is changing and growing all the time. We need to define continually who we each are and what we need from one another. Although it can be difficult and frightening to work out the conflict in such an intense relationship, the risk is worth it. Few bonds are as strong as that between a mother and a daughter; even in pain we can find strength in that bond.

"The commandment we have from him is this: those who love God must love their brothers and sisters also" (1 John 4:21). That goes for mothers and daughters, too!

Prayer: Our loving God, empower us to find in all of our many roles as women the courage and strength to do the work of love. Amen.

Kristy Arnesen Pullen
Valley Forge, Pennsylvania

The Princess and the Pea

"Strength and dignity are her clothing, and she laughs at the time to come. She opens her mouth with wisdom, and the teaching of kindness is on her tongue. She looks well to the ways of her household, and does not eat the bread of idleness. Her children rise up and call her happy."—Proverbs 31:25-28

The peas landed in the dishpan with contented pops, as if happy finally to be released from their dark green closets. Mary watched her mother out of the corner of her eye, and was afraid, for her mother's face was tired, her hands worn with work, her hair silvered by age.

As if sensing her daughter's concern, her mother turned and smiled at her. The smile lit up the mother's entire face, crinkling her eyes, momentarily chasing away the shadows of age that Mary had seen hovering around her.

"Have you ever wondered what it would be like to be a pea?" her mother asked mischievously.

Mary laughed. "No, have you?"

"Sometimes. I always wanted to be that both-

ersome little pea in that fairy tale, remember?
The one that kept the princess awake?"

"Yes, I remember. Why that particular pea?"
Mary asked.

"I don't know," replied her mother. "I've always been struck by the fact that even though it was small, and tiny, and seemingly insignificant, it still made a difference."

"Mother," Mary asked gently, "What's the matter?"

"Nothing," her mother answered.

Mary paused. "No one could ever fail to notice you," she said at last.

Mary noticed a sudden brightness in her mother's eyes.

"Thank you, Mary. I needed to hear that."

A comfortable silence fell between them, interrupted only by the jubilant yells of the popping peas.

Prayer: Dear God, may I never take for granted the woman who gave me life, who taught me love, who showed me what faith is all about. Amen.

Joyce Anderson-Reed
Fairbanks, Alaska

Days of Summer

" 'If you continue in my word, you are truly my disciples; and you will know the truth, and the truth will make you free.' "—John 8:31-32

Some of you may know the song about the "lazy, hazy, crazy days of summer" that the late Nat King Cole made famous in the early sixties. When I was a young child, it was one of my favorites. My sister and I used to pretend we were television celebrities, grab our mikes, (the ever popular ash tree twig—a big hit with our contemporaries), and sing that song to our hearts' content!

Summer was a season I always looked forward to as a young girl. It was a time of freedom—freedom from school and schedules. It was a time to bike and play outside until the late hours of the evening.

When the shadows of adolescence fell upon my shoulders, summer became a season of oppression. While my friends were buying two-piece bikinis, I was shopping around for a full-body wet suit! While my friends were finding every opportunity to be outside in the bright sunlight, I was writhing in terror at the idea of the sun's rays exposing my imperfect body.

120

By the age of thirteen, I was an excellent student of the "to be valuable, I must look beautiful" school of thought. Certainly watching the boyish Twiggy model miniskirts on the six o'clock news did little to help me accept my budding Rubenesque frame.

Many women struggle with body image and self-acceptance. Low self-esteem seems to be a prevalent side effect of being raised female in a glamour-crazed society.

The gospel message points to the truth that we are subjects of the creation of God and not objects to be abused by cultural expectations. We can escape the oppression we have learned by embracing the freedom of acceptance and salvation offered to us through Jesus.

Prayer: May the truth of your love, O God, give us the freedom to play shamelessly in the sun all the days of our lives. Amen.

Kathleen C. Busby
Waukegan, Illinois

A Whole New World

A whole new world opened up to me in the summer of 1978 during my first national American Baptist Women's conference at the American Baptist Assembly in Green Lake, Wisconsin. During vespers one evening, I became aware of our wonderful source of empowerment by the Holy Spirit. The leader's focus was spiritual gifts, and she quoted several times from Elizabeth O'Connor's book, *Eighth Day of Creation: Gifts and Creativity* (Word Books, 1971). The following seemed to speak directly to me at a time when I was feeling very inadequate to fill a new role:

We ask to know the will of God without guessing that His will is written into our very beings. We perceive that will when we discern our gifts. . . . Because our gifts carry us out into the world and make us participants in life, the uncovering of them is one of the most important tasks confronting any one of us. When we talk about being true to ourselves—being the persons we are intended to be—we are talking about gifts.

Beginning that moment, the identification, development, and use of spiritual gifts became a major focus for me as a leader in American Baptist Women's Ministries. I realized that I not only had to do this in my own life but also had the responsibility to help others do the same so that all of us, as members of the body of Christ, might become more and more the persons God intends us to be.

If you don't know what your unique gifts are, I encourage you to identify them and develop them. Study the Scripture's teachings on gifts (such as Romans 12:1-8), spend time thinking about what you like to do and what you do best. Ask other persons to help you identify your gifts, and do a prepared "gifts survey." Most importantly, ask God to reveal your gifts to you. A whole new world can be opened to you.

Prayer: We praise you, Lord, for your plan of empowerment for the body of Christ. Thank you for the uniqueness that is mine. Forgive me when I fail to unwrap your gifts to me, or when I wish I had different gifts. I rejoice in the blessings and opportunities that are mine today, and pray that I might be a blessing to someone else in a special way. I thank you and praise you in Jesus' name. Amen.

Marilyn Momose
West Lawn, Pennsylvania

Inside the Berry

"For the Lord does not see as mortals see; they look on the outward appearance, but the Lord looks on the heart."—1 Samuel 16:7

In the part of the country where I live, summer means strawberry time. It means a trip to the berry field or fruit store to buy some "just picked" berries. Before taking a bite, my mouth used to water as I'd look at the dark, red, juicy berry I held in my hand. However, I've discovered that sometimes when I bite into one of those beautiful berries, I've been deceived!

The strawberry reminds me again that I can't judge something from just the outside. One berry can be very sour, while another, quite wonderful. I can't know what it's really like until I get inside. So it is with our relationships with one another. To know who someone really is inside, we must be willing to take the risk to go beyond the superficial appearances.

This day, strive to care about the persons you meet. Take time to look beyond the surface and see within.

Prayer: Our Loving God, forgive us when we don't look deep enough, or don't care enough.

Show us how to love even more than we believe
we are able. Amen.

Pat Clemensen
Tacoma, Washington

New Beginnings

"Finally, beloved, whatever is true, whatever is honorable, whatever is just, whatever is pure, whatever is pleasing, whatever is commendable, if there is any excellence and if there is anything worthy of praise, think about these things."—Philippians 4:8

Labor Day is like New Year's Day. In fact, it is more like New Year's than the traditional day in January. I can't forget school starting, which I have begun over twenty-two times as student or teacher. Fall is my favorite season, and Labor Day symbolizes its beginning. There are coming changes from the dullness of summer's end— changes in the color, in the air, in the smells, in the clothes we wear.

As a poem written for an older adult says, "Give me courage to hold a garage sale of thoughts I don't need." Not only is this a time to start anew, but also it is a time to create newness of mind—to mend bridges, to outgrow grudges, and to give up old failures. It is a time to clean out the garage and turn our attention to new beginnings.

Prayer: Lord, give me courage to change and

start anew. Help me to think about things that are worthy of praise. Amen.

Glenda Young
Merriam, Kansas

The Balm of Beauty

"I want you to be free from anxieties."
—*1 Corinthians 7:32*

Fall is one of the most beautiful times of the year. The air is fresh and seems to sparkle. The intense heat of the summer is forgotten with the cool, bright days of fall. The leaves are brilliant colors and beautiful to behold, both on and off the trees. The smell of burning leaves and apples baking spices the air.

The beauty of this time of year is truly a gift from God. Let us use this seasonal gift to help us to be free from anxieties. Take a moment to look around you, enjoy the season, and cast your burdens onto the Lord.

Prayer: We thank you for a beautiful world that can help soothe our troubled minds. Amen.

Glenda Young
Merriam, Kansas

Columbus Day

"So I run straight toward the goal in order to win the prize, which is God's call through Christ Jesus to the life above."—Philippians 3:14 (GNB)

In 1492 Columbus "sailed the ocean blue," and the world, for better or worse, was changed. Sometimes we speak about the nature of journeys as being "outward" or "inward." In either case, the goals are for new discoveries and achievements.

We have many stories about men on journeys, but it may be difficult to think of as many women explorers. Dorothy, from *The Wizard of Oz,* is a wonderful tale of a woman on a personal quest. Let your imagination loose and turn the characters who accompanied Dorothy on the Yellow Brick Road into female companions. But first, do you recognize in yourself a Dorothy who seeks that "homey" feeling of being secure, loved, and affirmed? And that the wicked witch is a warlock, personifying tradition and prejudice and therefore attempting to block Dorothy's progress, trying to steal her power to persevere and succeed by coveting her ruby red shoes.

Women do not need to journey alone. We

can share the companionship of those who, like the "Lioness" in Dorothy's story, seek courage and assertiveness; the "Tin Woman" who seeks to own her feelings; and the "Straw Woman" who wants the affirmation that it is okay to be intelligent and to think as well as feel. They need each other's help, and they help each other's needs.

Like Dorothy, at some point in our lives, we are caught up in the tornado-like winds of personal growth and change. And like Dorothy, we are set down upon our own special road of discovery and accomplishment. With the help of our sisters (and a guardian angel or two), we shall faithfully make our own way and reach the prize of self-actualization that lies just over the rainbow of hope, dreams, and promise.

Prayer: Gracious God, help me to recognize the companions on my journey. Draw us closer so that we can arrive together. Amen.

Sarah L. Hallstrand
Chicago, Illinois

The Joy of Working

"But Jesus answered them, 'My Father is still working, and I also am working.'"—John 5:17

"Why do you want to work?" is a question I am asked frequently. It is a question asked of women who can "live off another." You see, I have adequate income shared with my husband, and I do not need the money.

But the question could be turned around: "Why do people not want to work?" There is joy in working. Work provides us with many benefits. Usefulness, purpose, higher self-esteem, money, relationships, and creative outlets are just a few of the advantages of professional employment.

We may forget these benefits when work is hard or boring. That is the time to ask yourself the question, "Why do you want to work?" And ask God to show you the benefits of working. Joy may come from God through the asking.

Prayer: For work and the strength to do it, we thank you, O God. Amen.

Glenda Young
Merriam, Kansas